Understanding Paragraphs

Illustrated by Danny Beck

To find Remedia products in a store near you, go to: **www.rempub.com/stores**

REMEDIA PUBLICATIONS   **SCOTTSDALE, ARIZONA**

Answer Key

Page 1 1. Camels have special features that help them survive in the desert. 2. double rows of eyelashes, hairy ear openings, nostrils that can close down 3. They lose body water very slowly and store fat in their humps. A paragraph is a group of sentences that work together to tell about a single topic or idea.

Page 2 1. A porcupine eats tree bark. 2. porcupine quills 3. what a porcupine eats

Page 3 1. I, S, I, I, S, S 2. ¶An insect's body is divided into three parts. Insects also have two sets of wings and a set of antennae. Another thing about insects is that they have six legs. ¶A spider's body is made up of two parts. It has eight legs instead of six. Spiders do not have wings or antennae.

Page 4 1. P, P, B, P, B, B 2. ¶Bill loves pizza. His favorite kind is pepperoni pizza. Bill could eat pizza for breakfast, lunch, and dinner. ¶Rick's favorite food is a hamburger. He likes pickle relish and onions on his burger. Rick once ate four hamburgers for lunch.

Page 5 1. C, D, D, C, D, C 2. ¶Dogs can be very fine pets. They will run, bark, and chase after sticks and balls. They are sometimes called man's best friend. ¶Cats also can be nice pets. They will purr when their backs are stroked. They like to play with balls of yarn and will chase mice.

Page 6 1. S, S, K, K, K, S, K 2. ¶Sarah is the best speller in her class. She almost always scores 100 on her tests. Last week she even spelled spaghetti correctly. ¶Kent is a whiz at math. He hardly ever misses a problem. The other students wish they could do math as well as Kent. Kent wishes he could spell as well as Sarah does.

Page 7 1. C, J, J, C, J, J, C 2. ¶A baby koala bear is called a cub. The mother carries the baby koala in her pouch for many months. Then the cub rides on her back. ¶A baby kangaroo is called a joey. A newborn joey is about the size of a bee. A joey has no fur at birth. It lives in the mother kangaroo's pouch for several months after birth.

Page 8 Line through: There are rain forests in the tropical zone. 1. It does not belong because it talks about rain forests in the tropical zone, not just the location of the zone. Line through: Magic shows are fun to watch. 2. The paragraph is about superstitious belief in magic in relation to solar eclipses, not about modern-day entertainment. Line through: Some things seem to happen for no reason at all. 3. contradicts the first sentence

Page 9 1. S, S, E, X, E, S, E 2. ¶Anacondas are very big and powerful water snakes. They may be over a foot thick and 25 feet long. The largest of them can easily squeeze a man or animal to death. ¶Anacondas eat only about once a month. That is because when they eat, their meals are huge. They are able to swallow an entire deer.

Page 10 1. D, E, E, D, X, D, E 2. ¶Long ago white men came to the New World. They found Indians raising tomatoes for food. Where the white men lived in Europe, tomatoes were unknown. ¶Later, people in Europe grew tomatoes but did not eat them. They were afraid they might be poison. They used tomatoes for decorations rather than food.

Page 11 1. W, W, X, C, W, C, C 2. ¶Animals whose body temperatures stay the same most of the time are warm-blooded. Cows, dogs and other mammals, and birds are warm-blooded animals. Their bodies sweat or pant to become cooler. ¶Animals whose body temperatures change with the temperature of the air or water around them are cold-blooded. Snakes, frogs, fish, and alligators are some of the cold-blooded animals. They may move to a shaded place to become cooler.

Page 12 1. C, X, C, B, B, B, B 2. ¶A big, black crow was high in an oak tree near Brad's house. It sat very still. ¶Brad opened his window and looked out. Just then the crow flapped its big wings. It flew right by the open window. Brad slammed the window shut in surprise.

Page 13 1. M, G, G, G, M, X, G 2. ¶Marty was a real show-off. He always thought he could do things better than anyone else. ¶One day, Marty bragged that he could make the biggest bubble with his gum. He blew the bubble bigger and bigger. All at once, the bubble broke. Marty had gum all over his face.

Page 14 1. 2, 3, 1   3, 2, 1   2, 1, 4, 3 ¶Cody stepped up to the plate. The pitcher threw the ball. Cody swung the bat. He hit a home run.

Page 15 1. 3, 5, 1, 4, 2, 7, 6 2. ¶Mrs. Grady had many things to do today. First she went grocery shopping. After bringing the groceries home, she went to the dentist. Mrs. Grady stopped at the post office after the dentist. The fourth thing she did was take her car to be washed. From the car wash, she drove to the bank and then to the drugstore. Finally Mrs. Grady went home and did her household chores.

Page 16 1. 1, 4, 6, 2, 3, 7, 5 ¶Birds like to eat seeds. They also eat tiny stones, or gravel. Birds eat gravel to help grind their food. They have no teeth to do this. When birds eat seeds and gravel, they mix together in the bird's gizzard. A gizzard is like a stomach. The seeds are mashed up and become food for the bird's body.

Page 17 1. 4, 2, 8, 1, 5, 3, 7, 6 2. ¶Cathy got on an airplane for the first time. She was a little afraid when the plane took off. Soon she felt safe as it flew smoothly in the sky. Cathy looked down at the trees. She saw cars moving far below her. Everything looked so small. Cathy was having a great time. The next time she flies, Cathy will not be afraid. The order of the sentences may vary.

Page 18 1. N, S, N, N, S, S 2. ¶Countries north of the equator have more heat and light in the summer. This is because the northern part of the earth is leaning toward the sun. The Fourth of July in the north can be very hot. ¶Countries south of the equator have less heat and light in the summer. This is because the southern part of the earth is leaning away from the sun. Countries in the southern half might have a blizzard on the Fourth of July.

Page 19 1. A, A, W, A, W, A, W 2. ¶You can tell how old a tree is by looking at its rings. Each year, trees build new layers of wood to make their trunks thicker. The layers are marked by rings. When a tree is cut down, you can count the rings to find its age. ¶You also can tell what the weather was like by a tree's rings. The ring will be thin if the weather has been bad because the tree hasn't grown much. If it has had a lot of warm, sunny weather and plenty of water, the ring will be thick.

Page 20 1. A, R, A, R, A, R, A 2. ¶Rhode Island is the smallest of the United States. It has an area of 1,214 miles. This little state is on the east side of the U.S. ¶Alaska is the largest of the United States. It has an area of 586,400 square miles. It could hold over 450 Rhode Islands. The big state is in the northwest and touches the Pacific Ocean.

Page 21 1. G, M, G, M, M, G, M 2. ¶My favorite time at the zoo was spent watching the monkeys. They were swinging from limb to limb on a big tree. One monkey lost its grip and fell on top of another one. They were lucky they didn't get hurt. ¶I also liked the giraffes. They have long legs, long necks, and very long tongues. It must be very painful for a giraffe to get a sore throat.

Page 22 1. W, T, W, T, T, W, T 2. ¶In the 1840's, thousands of Americans decided to move west to Oregon. Oregon had good land for farming. There were lots of trees for building new homes. ¶The trip to Oregon was slow. It took many months to get there. People traveled in covered wagons pulled by horses or oxen. One time, 120 wagons formed a wagon train and made the trip together.

Page 23 1. B, B, A, B, A, B, A, A 2. ¶Maria woke up feeling very sick. Maria's mom said she would have to stay in bed all day. Then she felt even worse because she would miss the baseball game at school. Without her good hitting, her team would probably lose. ¶Toni came to Maria's house after school to tell her they had won the game. Maria was surprised and a little hurt that they had won without her. She knew she had to be a good sport about Toni's news. Maria told Toni she was glad their team had won.

Page 24 1. F, B, A, B, B, F, A, B, F, A 2. ¶A beaver's home is called a lodge. The lodge has two rooms. One room is above water and one room is underwater. A beaver gets into its home by going through the underwater room into the above-water room. ¶A fox lives in a burrow. A burrow is a hole in the ground that the fox digs. The fox usually hides in the burrow during the day and comes out to hunt for food at night. ¶An ant's home is called a nest. The nest can become very large since thousands of ants may live together in a colony. Mounds can be seen where the ants pile the dirt while digging the many tunnels in their home.

Page 25 1. W, D, W, D, Q, Q, W, D, Q 2. ¶One kind of honeybee is called the worker. Workers gather nectar from flowers. These worker bees also wait on the queen. ¶Drones are male honeybees. Drones do not work. Also, drones do not sting. ¶The queen is larger than the other bees. The queen honeybee lays the eggs. All the bees of the hive hatch from these eggs.

Page 26 1. R, P, M, P, M, R, M, M, R 2. ¶Mount McKinley is the highest mountain in North America. It has an altitude of 20,320 feet. It is called "the top of the continent." Mount McKinley is located in Alaska. ¶The next highest peak in the U.S. is Mount Ranier. It is 14,410 feet high. Mount Ranier is in the state of Washington. ¶Pikes Peak is 14,110 feet high. It is located in Colorado.

Page 27 1. F, L, S, L, S, L, F, S, L, L 2. ¶A butterfly goes through very different stages of growth before becoming full-grown. In the first stage, it is an egg. The egg soon changes into another form. ¶In the second stage of development, the egg becomes a caterpillar. The caterpillar looks like a fat worm and may have horn-like growths on its back. The skin of the caterpillar is thin and is usually green or gray in color. ¶Next comes the pupa stage. The pupa is a case, or covering, for the butterfly that is growing inside. The pupa hangs onto a surface such as a twig or the bark of a tree. Finally the pupa case breaks open and the butterfly comes out.

Page 28 1. E, S, S, C, E, C, S, E, C 2. ¶In 1492, only scholars and adventurers believed the earth was round. Even kings thought the earth was flat. They believed it was possible to fall off the edge into space. ¶Columbus believed the earth was round. He wanted to sail around it. He was poor, though, and needed ships. ¶Finally the king and queen of Spain gave Columbus three ships. In return, any land or riches he found would belong to the queen. She hoped Columbus would make her very rich.

Page 29 1. L, F, J, F, L, J, F, L, F, L, J, L 2. ¶Fred could not find his math book. If he didn't find it, he would not get his homework done. Where could it be? ¶First Fred looked in the kitchen. He had gone there for a snack when he came home from school. It was not in the kitchen. Then Fred looked all around his bedroom. It wasn't in there either. ¶Finally Fred called his friend Josh. He and Josh had left school together. "I have your math book, Fred," said Josh. "I guess I picked it up by mistake."

Page 30 Paragraphs will vary.

Understanding Paragraphs

Name _____

What is a Paragraph?

   To help a reader understand or follow the line of thought in a story, article, news account, or report, a writer divides the information into parts called paragraphs. A paragraph is a group of sentences that work together to tell about a single topic or idea. When the writer moves on to another topic, or to different information about the same subject, it is put into a new paragraph. Each new paragraph is set off from the others by its first line which is indented, or started, a short distance from the left margin.

Read the paragraph; then answer the questions.

   Camels have special features that help them survive in the desert. They have double rows of eyelashes, hairy ear openings, and nostrils that can be closed down. All of these protect them from blowing sand. Camels also store fat in their humps. They lose body water very slowly. They can go for several days without any food or water.

1. The paragraph is about what topic?

   _____

2. What special features do camels have to protect them from sand?

   _____

   _____

3. Why can they go several days without food and water?

   _____

Complete the statement.

A paragraph is _____

_____

Name _____

Starting A New Paragraph

A paragraph tells about a single topic or idea. When more than one topic or idea is written about a subject, each new topic or idea is put in a separate paragraph.

The following article is about one subject--porcupines. It tells two different things about porcupines. The sentences that tell about one thing should be in one paragraph. The sentences that tell about the second thing should be in another paragraph.

Read the article. Decide where the second paragraph should begin.

The tail and body of a porcupine are covered with about 30,000 loosely attached quills. It cannot throw its quills, as some people claim. If the porcupine bats its enemy with its tail, though, the quills attach themselves to whatever they touch. A por-cupine eats tree bark. It also craves salt. Farmers sometimes find the wooden handles of their tools chewed off. The porcupine had found wood seasoned with the salt of human sweat.

1.   Write the first sentence of the second paragraph.

_____

2.   What is the topic of the first paragraph?

_____

3.   What is the topic of the second paragraph?

_____

Name _____

1. Read each sentence below. If the sentence tells about an insect, write an I on the line. If it tells about a spider, write an S on the line.

_____ An insect's body is divided into three parts.

_____ A spider's body is made up of two parts.

_____ Insects also have two sets of wings and a set of antennae.

_____ Another thing about insects is that they have six legs.

_____ It has eight legs instead of six.

_____ Spiders do not have wings or antennae.

2. Write each group of sentences in order to make two paragraphs. The first paragraph should tell about insects. The second one should tell about spiders.

Insects and Spiders

_____

_____

_____

_____

_____

_____

_____

_____

_____

Name _____

1. **Read each sentence below. If the sentence tells about pizza, write a P on the line. If it tells about a burger, write a B on the line.**

_____ Bill loves pizza.

_____ His favorite kind is pepperoni pizza.

_____ Rick's favorite food is a hamburger.

_____ Bill could eat pizza for breakfast, lunch, and dinner.

_____ He likes pickle relish and onions on his burger.

_____ Rick once ate four hamburgers for lunch.

2. **Write each group of sentences in order to make two paragraphs. The first paragraph should tell about pizza. The second one should tell about burgers.**

Pizzas or Burgers

_____

_____

_____

_____

_____

_____

_____

_____

_____

_____

Name _____

1. **Read each sentence below. If the sentence tells about dogs, write a D on the line. If it tells about cats, write a C on the line.**

_____ Cats also can be nice pets.

_____ Dogs can be very fine pets.

_____ They will run, bark, and chase after sticks or balls.

_____ They will purr when their backs are stroked.

_____ They are sometimes called man's best friend.

_____ They like to play with balls of yarn and will chase mice.

2. **Write each group of sentences in order to make two paragraphs. The first paragraph should tell about dogs. The second one should tell about cats.**

People Pals

_____

_____

_____

_____

_____

_____

_____

_____

_____

_____

Name _____

1. **Read each sentence below. If the sentence tells about Sarah, write an S on the line. If it tells about Kent, write a K on the line.**

_____ Sarah is the best speller in her class.

_____ She almost always scores 100 on her tests.

_____ Kent is a whiz at math.

_____ He hardly ever misses a problem.

_____ The other students wish they could do math as well as Kent.

_____ Last week she even spelled spaghetti correctly.

_____ Kent wishes he could spell as well as Sarah does.

2. **Write each group of sentences in order to make two paragraphs. The first paragraph should tell about Sarah. The second one should tell about Kent.**

Scholars

_____

_____

_____

_____

_____

_____

_____

_____

_____

_____

_____

 ©Remedia Publications

Name _____

1. **Read each sentence below. If the sentence tells about a joey, write a J on the line. If it tells about a cub, write a C on the line.**

_____ A baby koala bear is called a cub.

_____ A baby kangaroo is called a joey.

_____ A newborn joey is about the size of a bee.

_____ The mother carries the baby koala in her pouch for many months.

_____ A joey has no fur at birth.

_____ It lives in the mother kangaroo's pouch for several months after birth.

_____ Then the cub rides on her back.

2. **Write each group of sentences in order to make two paragraphs. The first paragraph should tell about a joey. The second one should tell about a cub.**

Animal Babies

_____

_____

_____

_____

_____

_____

_____

_____

_____

_____

_____

Name _____

Keeping To The Main Idea

A paragraph tells about a single topic or idea. Sentences that do not keep to the main idea of the paragraph can confuse the reader.

Read each paragraph. Draw a line through the sentence that does not keep to the main idea. Then explain why it does not belong in the paragraph.

The earth has five climate zones. The two polar zones are cold and icy. The hot and rainy tropical zone is around the equator. There are rain forests in the tropical zone. Two temperate zones are between the tropical and polar zones.

1. Why it does not belong: _____

A long time ago, when people couldn't explain something, they called it magic. When the sun was blacked out during an eclipse, they thought magic caused it to happen. We now know a solar eclipse is caused by the moon passing between the earth and sun. Magic shows are fun to watch.

2. Why it does not belong: _____

Scientists say there is a logical reason for everything. Some things seem to happen for no reason at all. Physicists call this *cause and effect*. For instance, if something moves across the floor, there must be a force that caused it to move.

3. Why it does not belong: _____

Name _____

1. **Read each sentence below. If the sentence tells about the size and strength of the anacondas, write an S on the line. If it tells about their eating habits, write an E on the line. If the sentence does not keep to the topics, put an X on the line.**

_____ Anacondas are very big and powerful water snakes.

_____ They may be over a foot thick and 25 feet long.

_____ Anacondas eat only about once a month.

_____ It would be scary to meet an anaconda.

_____ That is because when they eat, their meals are huge.

_____ The largest of them can easily squeeze a man or animal to death.

_____ They are able to swallow an entire deer.

2. **Write each group of sentences in order to make two paragraphs. The first paragraph should tell about size. The second one should tell about eating habits.**

Anacondas

_____

_____

_____

_____

_____

_____

_____

_____

_____

_____

_____

Name _____

1. **Read each sentence below. If the sentence tells about discovering tomatoes, write a D on the line. If it tells how people in Europe used tomatoes, write an E on the line. If the sentence does not keep to the topics, put an X on the line.**

_____ Long ago white men came to the New World.

_____ Later, people in Europe grew tomatoes but did not eat them.

_____ People were afraid they might be poison.

_____ They found Indians raising tomatoes for food.

_____ Tomatoes taste good in a salad.

_____ Where the white men lived in Europe, tomatoes were unknown.

_____ They used tomatoes for decorations rather than food.

2. **Write each group of sentences in order to make two paragraphs. The first paragraph should tell about discovering tomatoes. The second one should tell about how Europeans used them. Do not include the X sentence.**

Mystery Fruit

_____

_____

_____

_____

_____

_____

_____

_____

_____

_____

_____

Name _____

1. **Read each sentence below. If the sentence tells about cold-blooded animals, write a C on the line. If it tells about warm-blooded animals, write a W on the line. If the sentence does not keep to the topics, put an X on the line.**

_____ Animals whose body temperatures stay the same most of the time are warm-blooded.

_____ Cows, dogs and other mammals, and birds are warm-blooded animals.

_____ Dogs swim in order to cool themselves.

_____ Animals whose body temperatures change with the temperature of the air or water around them are cold-blooded.

_____ Their bodies sweat or pant to become cooler.

_____ Snakes, frogs, fish, and alligators are some of the cold-blooded animals.

_____ They may move to a shaded place to become cooler.

2. **Write each group of sentences in order to make two paragraphs. The first paragraph should tell about warm-blooded animals. The second one should tell about cold-blooded animals. Do not include the X sentence.**

Warm Blood - Cold Blood

_____

_____

_____

_____

_____

_____

_____

_____

_____

_____

_____

Name _____

1. **Read each sentence below. If the sentence tells about the crow in the tree, write a C on the line. If it tells about Brad and how the crow surprised him, write a B on the line. If the sentence does not keep to the topics, put an X on the line.**

_____ A big, black crow was high in an oak tree near Brad's house.

_____ Brad lives in a big house.

_____ It sat very still.

_____ Brad opened his window and looked out.

_____ Just then the crow flapped its big wings.

_____ It flew right by the open window.

_____ Brad slammed the window shut in surprise.

2. **Write each group of sentences in order to make two paragraphs. The first paragraph should tell about the crow in the tree. The second one should tell about Brad and what the bird did to surprise him. Do not include the X sentence.**

Surprise!

_____

_____

_____

_____

_____

_____

_____

_____

_____

_____

_____

1. **Read each sentence below. If the sentence tells about what kind of boy Marty was, write an M on the line. If it tells what happened to Marty and his gum, write a G on the line. If the sentence does not keep to the topics, put an X on the line.**

    _____ Marty was a real show-off.

    _____ One day, Marty bragged that he could make the biggest bubble with his gum.

    _____ He blew the bubble bigger and bigger.

    _____ All at once, the bubble broke.

    _____ He always thought he could do things better than anyone else.

    _____ Peppermint-flavored bubble gum tastes the best.

    _____ Marty had gum all over his face.

2. **Write each group of sentences in order to make two paragraphs. The first paragraph should tell what kind of boy Marty was. The second one should tell what happened when Marty blew a gum bubble. Do not include the X sentence.**

Bubble Trouble

_____

_____

_____

_____

_____

_____

_____

_____

_____

_____

Keeping Order

Paragraphs that tell about events, give directions, or tell a story should be written in the right order. That means the sentences should be in the order that they happened or should happen.

Example:

<u>Out of Order</u>	<u>Correct Order</u>
She fell asleep	Tracy put on pajamas
Tracy put on pajamas	She got into bed.
She got into bed.	She fell asleep.

1. **Number each set of sentences so they are in the correct order.**

   _____ Toast the bread.   _____ Then rain poured down.

   _____ Butter the toast.   _____ It started to sprinkle.

   _____ Put bread in toaster.   _____ Dark clouds appeared.

2. **Number the sentences in the correct order. Then write a paragraph putting the sentences in the right order.**

   _____ The pitcher threw the ball.

   _____ Cody stepped up to the plate.

   _____ He hit a home run.

   _____ Cody swung the bat.

_____

_____

_____

_____

14

Name _____

1. **The sentences about Mrs. Grady's day are not in the right order. Number the sentences in their correct order.**

_____ After bringing the groceries home, she went to the dentist.

_____ The fourth thing she did was take her car to be washed.

_____ Mrs. Grady had many things to do today.

_____ Mrs. Grady stopped at the post office after the dentist.

_____ First, she went grocery shopping.

_____ Finally Mrs. Grady went home and did her household chores.

_____ From the car wash, she drove to the bank and then to the drugstore.

2. **Now write one paragraph putting the sentences in their correct order.**

Mrs. Grady's Busy Day

_____

_____

_____

_____

_____

_____

_____

_____

_____

_____

Name _____

1. **The sentences about birds are not in the right order. Number the sentences in their correct order.**

_____ Birds like to eat seeds.

_____ They have no teeth to do this.

_____ A gizzard is like a stomach.

_____ They also eat tiny stones, or gravel.

_____ Birds eat gravel to help grind their food.

_____ The seeds are mashed up and become food for the bird's body.

_____ When birds eat seeds and gravel, they mix together in the bird's gizzard.

2. **Now write one paragraph putting the sentences in their correct order.**

Gravel Teeth

_____

_____

_____

_____

_____

_____

_____

_____

_____

_____

Name _____

1. The sentences about Cathy's plane ride are not in the right order. Number the sentences in their correct order.

_____ Cathy looked down at the trees.

_____ She was a little afraid when the plane took off.

_____ The next time she flies, Cathy will not be afraid.

_____ Cathy got on an airplane for the first time.

_____ She saw cars moving far below her.

_____ Soon she felt safe as it flew smoothly in the sky.

_____ Cathy was having a great time.

_____ Everything looked so small.

2. Now write one paragraph putting the sentences in their correct order.

High in the Sky

_____

_____

_____

_____

_____

_____

_____

_____

_____

_____

_____

Name _____

1. Read each sentence below. If the sentence tells about the north, write an N on the line. If it tells about the south, write an S on the line.

_____ This is because the northern part of the earth is leaning toward the sun.

_____ Countries in the southern half might have a blizzard on the Fourth of July.

_____ Countries north of the equator have more heat and light in the summer.

_____ The Fourth of July in the north can be very hot.

_____ This is because the southern part of the earth is leaning away from the sun.

_____ Countries south of the equator have less heat and light in the summer.

2. Put each group of sentences in the correct order to write two paragraphs. You may want to number them before writing your paragraphs.

Snow on the Fourth of July

_____

_____

_____

_____

_____

_____

_____

_____

_____

_____

18

Name _____

1. **Read each sentence below. If the sentence tells about the age of a tree, write an A on the line. If it tells about the weather, write a W on the line.**

_____ You can tell how old a tree is by looking at its rings.

_____ Each year trees build new layers of wood to make their trunks thicker.

_____ You also can tell what the weather was like by a tree's rings.

_____ The layers are marked by rings.

_____ The ring will be thin if the weather has been bad because the tree hasn't grown much.

_____ When a tree is cut down, you can count the rings to find its age.

_____ If it has had a lot of warm, sunny weather and plenty of water, the ring will be thick.

2. **Write each group of sentences in order to make two paragraphs. The first paragraph should tell about a tree's age; the second paragraph should be about the weather. You may want to number the sentences before writing your paragraphs.**

99 Years Old

_____

_____

_____

_____

_____

_____

_____

_____

_____

_____

Name _____

1. **Read each sentence below. If the sentence is about Rhode Island, write an R on the line. If it is about Alaska, write an A on the line.**

_____ It has an area of 586,400 square miles.

_____ This little state is on the east side of the U.S.

_____ Alaska is the largest of the United States.

_____ It has an area of 1,214 square miles.

_____ It could hold over 450 Rhode Islands.

_____ Rhode Island is the smallest of the United States.

_____ The big state is in the northwest and touches the Pacific Ocean.

RHODE ISLAND

ALASKA

2. **Put each group of sentences in the correct order to write two paragraphs. The first paragraph should tell about Rhode Island; the second, Alaska. You may want to number them before writing your paragraphs.**

Little and Big

_____

_____

_____

_____

_____

_____

_____

_____

_____

_____

_____

Name _____

1. **Read each sentence below. If the sentence tells about monkeys, write an M on the line. If it tells about giraffes, write a G on the line.**

    _____ I also liked the giraffes.

    _____ They were swinging from limb to limb on a big tree.

    _____ It must be very painful for a giraffe to get a sore throat.

    _____ My favorite time at the zoo was spent watching the monkeys.

    _____ One monkey lost its grip and fell on top of another one.

    _____ They have long legs, long necks, and very long tongues.

    _____ They were lucky they didn't get hurt.

2. **Put each group of sentences in the correct order to write two paragraphs. The first paragraph should tell about monkeys; the second, giraffes. You may want to number them before writing your paragraphs.**

Fun at the Zoo

_____

_____

_____

_____

_____

_____

_____

_____

_____

_____

_____

Name _____

1. **Read each sentence about early Americans moving west. If the sentence tells about when and why people wanted to go to Oregon, write a W on the line. If it tells about the trip itself, write a T on the line.**

_____ In the 1840's, thousands of Americans decided to move west to Oregon.

_____ The trip to Oregon was slow.

_____ Oregon had good land for farming.

_____ One time, 120 wagons formed a wagon train and made the trip together.

_____ It took many months to get there.

_____ There were lots of trees for building new homes.

_____ People traveled in covered wagons pulled by horses or oxen.

2. **Write each group of sentences in the correct order to make two paragraphs. The first paragraph should tell about when and why the trip was made; the second, about the trip itself. You may want to number the sentences before writing your paragraph.**

Wagons West!

_____

_____

_____

_____

_____

_____

_____

_____

_____

_____

Name _____

1. **Read each sentence about a baseball game. If the sentence is about Maria before the game, write a B on the line. If it tells about Maria after the game, write an A on the line.**

_____ Maria woke up feeling very sick.

_____ Without her good hitting, her team would probably lose.

_____ Maria was surprised and a little hurt that they had won without her.

_____ Maria's mom said she would have to stay in bed all day.

_____ Toni came to Maria's house after school to tell her they had won the game.

_____ Then she felt even worse because she would miss the baseball game at school.

_____ She knew she had to be a good sport about Toni's news.

_____ Maria told Toni she was glad their team had won.

2. **Write each group of sentences in the correct order to make two paragraphs. The first paragraph should tell about Maria before the game; the second paragraph should be about Maria after the game. You may want to number the sentences before writing your paragraphs.**

The Baseball Game

_____

_____

_____

_____

_____

_____

_____

_____

_____

_____

Home Sweet Home

1. **Read each sentence about animals' homes. If the sentence tells about a beaver's home, put a B on the line. If it tells about a fox's home, put an F on the line. If it tells about an ant's home, put an A on the line.**

_____ A fox lives in a burrow.

_____ The lodge has two rooms.

_____ The nest can become very large since thousands of ants may live together in a colony.

_____ A beaver's home is called a lodge.

_____ One room is above water and one room is underwater.

_____ A burrow is a hole in the ground that the fox digs.

_____ An ant's home is called a nest.

_____ A beaver gets into its home by going through the underwater room into the above-water room.

_____ The fox usually hides in the burrow during the day and comes out to hunt for food at night.

_____ Mounds can be seen where the ants pile the dirt while digging the many tunnels in their home.

2. **On a separate sheet of paper, write three paragraphs using the above sentences. The first paragraph should tell about a beaver's home. The second paragraph should tell about a fox's home, and the third, about an ant's home. Number each of the sentences in their correct order before writing your paragraphs.**

Busy Bees

1. **Read each sentence about honeybees. If the sentence tells about workers, put a W on the line. If it tells about drones, put a D on the line. If it tells about the queen, put a Q on the line.**

    _____ These worker bees also wait on the queen.

    _____ Drones do not work.

    _____ Also, drones do not sting.

    _____ The queen honeybee lays the eggs.

    _____ All the bees of the hive hatch from these eggs.

    _____ Workers gather nectar from flowers.

    _____ Drones are male honeybees.

    _____ The queen is larger than the other bees.

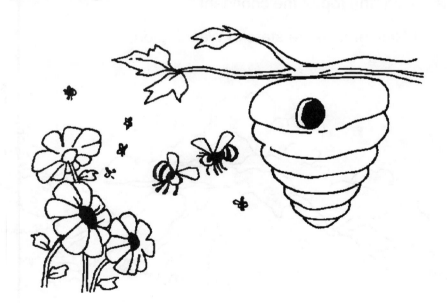

2. **On a separate sheet of paper, write three paragraphs using the above sentences. The first paragraph should tell about worker bees. The second paragraph should tell about drones, and the third, about the queen. Number each of the sentences in their correct order before writing your paragraphs.**

King of the Mountain

1. **Read each sentence. If the sentence is about Mount McKinley, put an M on the line. If it is about Mount Rainier, put an R on the line. If it is about Pikes Peak, put a P on the line.**

_____ It is 14,410 feet high.

_____ Pikes Peak is 14,110 feet high.

_____ Mount McKinley is the highest mountain in North America.

_____ It is located in Colorado.

_____ It has an altitude of 20,320 feet.

_____ The next highest peak in the U.S. is Mount Rainier.

_____ Mount McKinley is located in Alaska.

_____ It is called "the top of the continent."

_____ Mount Rainier is in the state of Washington.

2. **On a separate sheet of paper, write three paragraphs using the above sentences. The first paragraph should tell about Mount McKinley. The second paragraph should tell about Mount Rainier, and the third, about Pikes Peak. Number each of the sentences in their correct order before writing your paragraphs.**

Birth of a Butterfly

1. **Read each sentence about the growth of a butterfly. If the sentence tells about a butterfly's growth and first stage, write an F on the line. If it tells about the second stage, write an S on the line. If it tells about the last stage write an L on the line.**

_____ In the first stage, it is an egg.

_____ Finally the pupa case breaks open and the butterfly comes out.

_____ The caterpillar looks like a fat worm and may have horn-like growths on its back.

_____ A butterfly goes through very different stages of growth before becoming full-grown.

_____ In the second stage of development, the egg becomes a caterpillar.

_____ At this time, the pupa does not eat much.

_____ The egg soon changes into another form.

_____ The skin of the caterpillar is thin and is usually green or gray in color.

_____ The pupa is a case, or covering, for the butterfly that is growing inside.

2. **On a separate sheet of paper, write three paragraphs using the above sentences. The first paragraph should tell about the first stage of growth. The second paragraph should tell about the second stage, and the third, about the final stage. Number each of the sentences in their correct order before writing your paragraphs.**

Name _____

Around the World

1. **Read each sentence about Columbus. If the sentence tells what people thought about the earth, write an E on the line. If it tells about Columbus and his wish to sail, write a C on the line. If it tells about the king or queen of Spain, write an S on the line.**

_____ In 1492, only scholars and adventurers believed the earth was round.

_____ Finally the king and queen of Spain gave Columbus three ships.

_____ She hoped Columbus would make her very rich.

_____ Columbus believed the earth was round.

_____ Even kings thought the earth was flat.

_____ He wanted to sail around it.

_____ In return, any land or riches he found would belong to the queen.

_____ They believed it was possible to fall off the edge into space.

_____ He was poor, though, and needed ships.

2. **On a separate sheet of paper, write three paragraphs using the above sentences. The first paragraph should tell about what people believed about the earth. The second paragraph should tell about Columbus, and the third, about the king or queen of Spain. Number each of the sentences in their correct order before writing your paragraphs.**

The Missing Math Book

1. **Read each sentence about Fred. If the sentence tells about Fred losing his math book, write an F on the line. If it tells about where he looked for it, write an L on the line. If it tells about his call to Josh, write a J on the line.**

_____ First, Fred looked in the kitchen.

_____ If he didn't find it, he would not get his homework done.

_____ "I have your math book, Fred," said Josh.

_____ Fred could not find his math book.

_____ He had gone there for a snack when he came home from school.

_____ Finally Fred called his friend Josh.

_____ Where could it be?

_____ It was not in the kitchen.

_____ He and Josh had left school together.

_____ It wasn't in his room either.

_____ "I guess I picked it up by mistake."

_____ Then Fred looked all around his bedroom.

2. **On a separate sheet of paper, write three paragraphs using the above sentences. The first paragraph should tell about Fred losing his book. Then write about the places he looked for it. End with his phone call to Josh. Number each of the sentences in their correct order before writing your paragraphs.**

Understanding Paragraphs

Name _____

Write two paragraphs on one of the following topics. Write three or more sentences in each paragraph.

Food: Describe your favorite food and a food you do not like.

Weekend: Tell what you like to do on Saturday and Sunday.

Luck: Tell about the luckiest thing that happened to you and the worst thing that happened to you.

Movies: Write about two good movies you have seen.

School: Write about your best subject and your hardest subject.

Pets: Write about two funny things that happened to your pet or pets.

Write three paragraphs on one of the following topics. Write three or more sentences in each paragraph.

Sports: Tell about three different sports you like.

Treasures: Write about three things that you treasure and why they are important to you.

Chores: Describe three chores you do at home.

Friends: Tell about three friends and why you like them.

Visits: Describe three interesting places you have visited.

A floating message: You are walking on a beach. Suddenly you see a bottle floating toward you on the water. There is a message in it.